AYO'S **AWESOME** ADVENTURES
IN

THE WINDY CITY

www.worldbook.com

World Book, Inc.
180 North LaSalle Street
Suite 900
Chicago, Illinois 60601
USA

For information about other World Book publi-cations, visit our website at www.worldbook.com or call 1-800-WORLDBK (967-5325).

For information about sales to schools and libraries, call 1-800-975-3250 (United States), or 1-800-837-5365 (Canada).

Library of Congress Cataloging-in-Publication Data for this volume has been applied for.

Ayo's Awesome Adventures
ISBN: 978-0-7166-3636-6 (set, hc.)

Ayo's Awesome Adventures in Chicago:
The Windy City
ISBN: 978-0-7166-3640-3 (hc.)

Also available as:
ISBN: 978-0-7166-3651-9 (e-book)

1st printing July 2018

Staff

Contents

Introduction. 4

Chicago River. 8

Historic Water Tower 10

Skyscrapers. 12

Art Institute of Chicago 14

Millennium Park 16

Navy Pier 18

Museum Campus. 20

Lakefront Trail. 24

Lakefront beaches. 26

Lincoln Park Zoo 28

Peggy Notebaert Nature Museum 30

Sports town 32

Baseball 34

Blues. 36

Chicago eats 38

Museum of Science and Industry 40

Robie House. 42

Postcards from Chicago 44

Glossary 46

Acknowledgments 46

Index 47

For further reading 48

Introduction

Are you ready for an adventure? My name is Ayo. I'm an aardvark, an African mammal that eats ants and termites. I'm also a tour guide traveling the world. I hope you will come with me. We are going to explore cities around the globe. In this book, we will visit Chicago. Chicago is the third largest city in the United States, in the middle of the

continent of North America. Only New York City and Los Angeles, in California, have more people than Chicago. Aren't you curious about my name? *Ayo* is an African word that means *joy*.

We will see many things and places on our travels. Some of them may not be familiar to you. I'll try to explain any words you don't know. If I can explain them easily, I'll do so right where you are reading. Some words cannot be explained very easily. Or, I may use them over and over again. In that case, I will put them in boldface. Boldface is type that **looks like this.** All boldface words are defined in a glossary in the back of the book.

Some names and words may also be hard to say. I'll try to sound them out. Let's try this one. Chicago is known for its *architecture,* the design of its buildings. That's a big word! It is said *AHR kuh TEHK chur.*

You will probably want to tell others about our trip to Chicago. Then you can use the new words you learn. You will sound quite smart!

I hope someday you can travel with your family to Chicago. You can ask to see the places we visit in this book! Then you can be the tour guide for your parents and brothers and sisters.

Chicago information

- Population: 2,695,598

- Founded: 1803

- Transportation hub: Chicago has been the center of a huge transportation network since the 1800's. Vast railyards brought goods and people to ports on Lake Michigan and the Chicago River system. Today, the city has one of the world's busiest airports.

- Nickname: Chicago is called the *Windy City* because its residents like to brag. (Read more about it on page 19!)

United States information

- Climate: The U.S. Midwest region, which includes Chicago, has warm summers and cold, snowy winters.

- Money: U.S. dollar. One hundred cents equal one dollar.

- Flag: 50 white stars, for the 50 U.S. states, and 13 red and white stripes, for the original 13 American Colonies

flag of the United States

Chicago River

I am excited to show you Chicago! Let's start with the Chicago River. It runs through the heart of the city. I see something new every time I take a cruise on the river. Let's grab a seat on the top deck of the boat. We will see skyscrapers all around us.

Native Americans were the first people to live in this area. Wild onions used to grow along the riverbanks. The name *Chicago* comes from a Native American word for wild onions.

Native Americans called the Potawatomi traveled on the river hundreds of years ago. They paddled their canoes on the river to meet other nearby Native Americans. The people would trade—give and get things—with one another. In 1803, the U.S. government built Fort Dearborn, at the place where Michigan Avenue now crosses the river. Traders and farmers settled around it. The settlement grew to become the city.

Bridges can rise up along the Chicago River, allowing tall sailboats to pass underneath. The bridges are raised in the spring to allow boats to enter Lake Michigan. In the fall, they are raised so that boats can return to storage.

The river flows backward! Until 1900, the Chicago River flowed into Lake Michigan. But wastes in the river dirtied the lake, where the city got its drinking water. **Engineers** came up with a way to make the river flow backward. It has flowed away from the lake ever since!

Historic Water Tower

Our next stop is on Michigan Avenue. Fancy, modern buildings line this part of the avenue, called the "Magnificent Mile." But one building looks different. Can you spot the historic Water Tower? It looks a little like a tower in a fairy tale.

The Water Tower and the pumping station across the street were built in 1869. Inside them is part of the pipe system that pumped the city's water from Lake Michigan. One of the pipes was really tall. The water tower was built around it.

In October 1871, the Great Chicago Fire swept through downtown. Most of the city was made of wood and easily burned. The water tower and pumping station are made out of limestone. They were two of the few downtown buildings that survived!

Legend says that the fire was started by a cow that belonged to a woman named Mrs. O'Leary. The cow kicked over a lantern, starting the fire. No one knows for sure how the fire really started. But it killed about 300 people and destroyed one-third of the city. Almost 100,000 people lost their homes.

Chicago's flag has two blue stripes and four red stars. Each star stands for an important event in the city's history. One star is for the Great Chicago Fire.

The Great
Chicago Fire

Skyscrapers

The skyscraper was invented in Chicago! The Great Chicago Fire in 1871 destroyed much of downtown. But it wasn't long before **architects** and **engineers** drew up plans for new buildings.

They designed buildings with frames of steel covered in stone. No wood this time! They also planned buildings to rise up instead of spread out. An architect named William Le Baron Jenney designed the Home Insurance Building in the early 1880's. It rose 10 stories into the sky. You might not think that's very tall. But back then, it was amazing. The building was torn down in 1931. But the steel frame design that made it famous is still used around the world today.

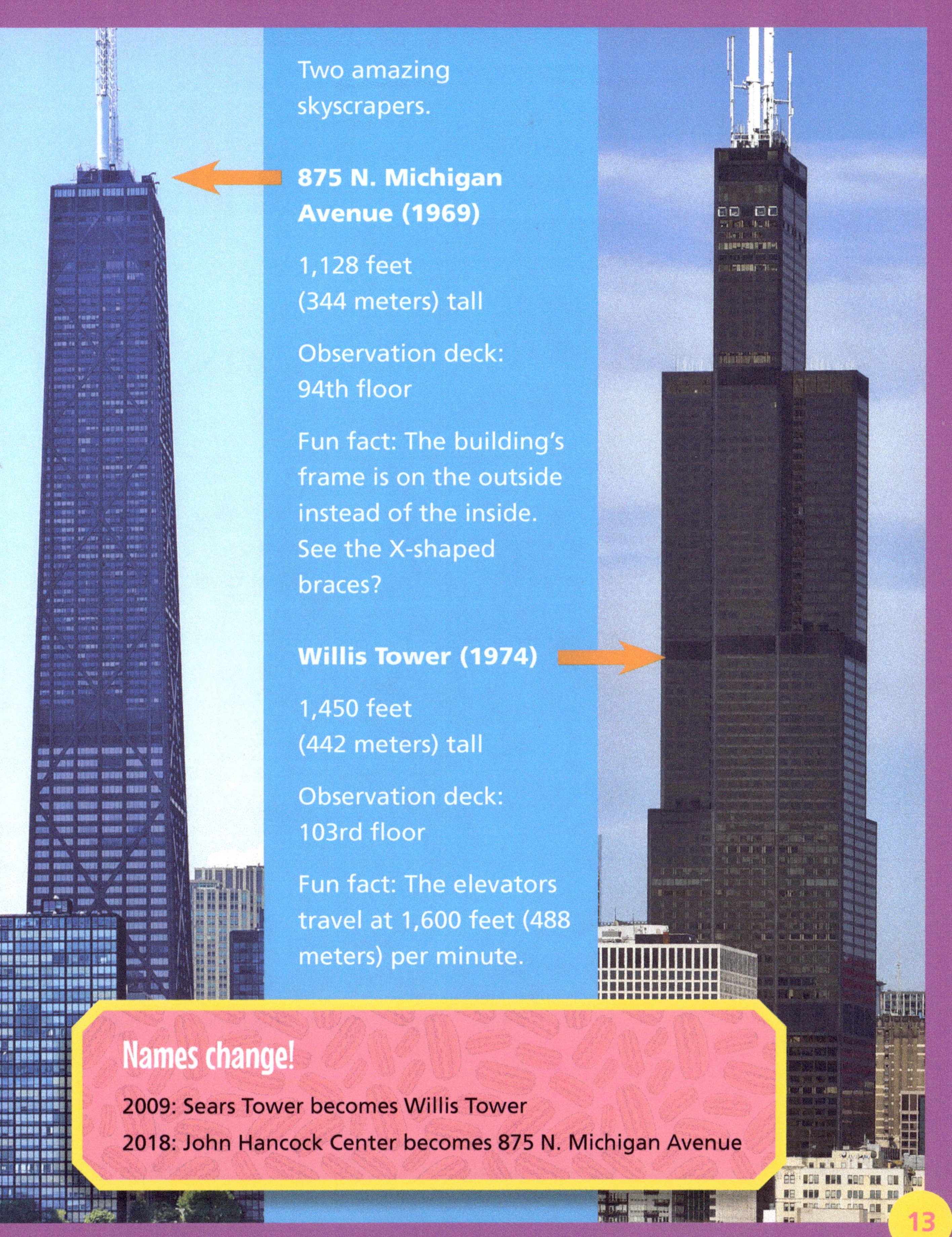

Two amazing skyscrapers.

875 N. Michigan Avenue (1969)

1,128 feet (344 meters) tall

Observation deck: 94th floor

Fun fact: The building's frame is on the outside instead of the inside. See the X-shaped braces?

Willis Tower (1974)

1,450 feet (442 meters) tall

Observation deck: 103rd floor

Fun fact: The elevators travel at 1,600 feet (488 meters) per minute.

Names change!

2009: Sears Tower becomes Willis Tower

2018: John Hancock Center becomes 875 N. Michigan Avenue

Art Institute of Chicago

The heart of downtown Chicago is called the **Loop.** That's where we'll find the Art Institute, a giant art museum. Huge statues of lions guard the entrance.

Inside the museum, you can see many famous paintings. One of the most famous is *A Sunday Afternoon on the Island of La Grande Jatte* by the French artist Georges Seurat. (You say that name *zhawrzh suh RAH.*) This huge painting shows a park scene. If you look closely, you will see the picture is made up of millions of tiny hand-painted dots. It took two years to paint!

There are more than just paintings at the Art Institute. Don't forget to check out their collection of arms and armor from medieval and Renaissance times (the 400's to the 1500's). You'll see swords, armor, and other weapons used by knights, soldiers, and hunters. There are even two life-sized warriors on horseback.

The Loop is where we'll see lots of skyscrapers, theaters, and business people. Do you see the **L** (elevated train) tracks above the street? They make a loop in the heart of the city, giving the area its name.

Millennium Park

A quick—but careful—hop across the street brings us to the Lurie Garden. What a delightful green place! Butterflies flap and honey bees buzz among the **prairie** plants! The garden is part of Millennium Park. Visitors come to the park for picnics, outdoor concerts, garden walks, and splashing in fountains.

Two tall towers stand in the park's Crown Fountain. The towers are covered in clear glass bricks. The bricks are lit from within by special lights called LED's. The LED's glow in various colors. Some of them shine giant pictures of the faces of **Chicagoans.** Water sprays from the towers, looking like it's being spit from the mouths of the faces. It looks funny, and it feels cool on a hot day!

Get your camera ready for the Bean! It is a huge, bean-shaped sculpture that looks great in photos. The sculpture's real name is *Cloud Gate.* Its shiny metal surface reflects the Chicago skyline and whatever silly faces we make when we stand close to it.

Parks and other outdoor spaces just keep stretching in front of us! Next to this park is Maggie Daley Park, then Grant Park, then the Museum Campus, and more to the south and north. Parks help keep the city's Lake Michigan shoreline open for everyone to enjoy.

Navy Pier

A quick bus ride will take us over the Chicago River and out to Navy Pier. It's easy to find. Just look for the huge Ferris wheel. Let's ride it! This Ferris wheel has cars that close completely, so we can ride it even in winter. As we rise, check out the great views of the skyline. You can also see the rest of the pier stretching into Lake Michigan!

Navy Pier didn't always have rides, theaters, restaurants, and boat cruises. It was built in 1916. Then it was used by passenger ships and cargo ships that traveled the lake. Navy Pier doesn't handle cargo ships today. But, freighters and barges

still pass through Chicago. They carry such things as steel, iron ore, and wheat. The city's rivers link the Great Lakes and the Mississippi River. Boats can get from here to the Atlantic Ocean! The Port of Chicago is one of the country's busiest.

Can you feel the wind in your fur?

Lots of people call Chicago the Windy City, but not because of the wind. **Chicagoans** have always been proud of their city and so became known for bragging about it during the 1893 Columbian Exposition. This habit led the city to be called *windy,* meaning *boastful* or *bragging.*

Museum Campus

From Navy Pier, we can see our next stop, the Museum Campus. The campus is a park where there are some big attractions. But how do we get there? Because it is summer, we can take a boat called a water taxi!

The water taxi drops us off at John G. Shedd Aquarium, on the Lake Michigan shore. There, we can see fish and other water-living creatures from around the world. Let me introduce you to the largest fish in Lake Michigan, the lake sturgeon. It can grow as long as 9 feet (3 meters). That's the distance from your bedroom floor to the ceiling. We'll also meet turtles, coral reef fish, beluga whales, and playful otters.

Next door, at the Field Museum, we can say hi to Sue. She's the largest nearly complete skeleton of *Tyrannosaurus rex*—a type of dinosaur—ever discovered. She is longer and taller than a school bus. Have you ever seen a mummy up close? Follow me into the ancient Egyptian tomb to see a big collection of them. We'll learn how mummies were made.

The Shedd and the Field

look like Greek temples, don't they? The same group of **architects** designed both buildings in the early 1900's.

Our last stop on the Museum Campus is the Adler Planetarium. It's a great place to learn about outer space! Do you ever lie on your back and look at the stars? In the planetarium's sky theater, we can sit back in total darkness and see pictures so realistic that it feels like we're flying between galaxies. I never knew there were so many neat things in outer space!

Before we go, let's check out the Gemini 12 spacecraft. Astronauts rode it into orbit around Earth. I bet we could see Africa from orbit! If the weather is just right, we can also

look at the sun through the Doane Observatory telescope.

Whew! I need a break. Good thing the planetarium is next to Northerly Island Park, a nature preserve. Let's go for a walk on the winding paths or swim at the sandy 12th Street Beach. From here, we can look north to the skyscrapers that make up the city's skyline. Northerly Island is really a peninsula—land surrounded by water on three sides. It used to be a small airport with one runway. Imagine landing a plane so close to the water on this tiny strip of land!

Lakefront Trail

You may have noticed lots of bicycles around the lakefront parks and the Museum Campus. Many people bike the Lakefront Trail, a paved pathway along the shore of Lake Michigan. It runs way up to the North Side, way past Navy Pier, and way south, past the Museum of Science and Industry. It stretches 18 miles (29 kilometers)!

Look over one shoulder, and you will see parks and tall buildings. Look the other way for sandy beaches along Lake Michigan. Wow! The lake is so huge that we can't see the other side. It seems like we're next to the ocean!

There are so many fun places to stop for a swim or sightseeing! In summertime, Buckingham Fountain in Grant Park is hard to miss. It shoots water 150 feet (45 meters) into the air … as high as the Statue of Liberty. Eeek! We're downwind—and getting sprayed by water from the fountain!

Check out the Riverwalk for a different shoreline stroll. This path runs next to the Chicago River, on its south bank. We'll go underneath some of the city's famous lifting bridges! If it's hot, let's stop for *gelato*, a rich Italian-style ice cream.

Lakefront beaches

On hot summer days, I love feeling the sand between my claws! Chicago has lots of sandy beaches along Lake Michigan. They are connected by the Lakefront Trail. Let's go!

I like to swim and play volleyball at Oak Street Beach and North Avenue Beach. The North Avenue Beach House is shaped like a steamboat. They sell ice cream there. Yum!

Many Chicago beaches used to be really narrow until the 1920's. Then the city added to the shoreline, dumping sand along the lake. Barges hauled the sand from the Indiana Dunes—big hills of sand— across the lake. The city has also built *breakwater* barriers. These offshore walls of rock and other material protect the shoreline from being washed away by waves.

Lincoln Park Zoo

It's time to visit my favorite place in any city—the zoo! Let's cross this foot bridge over busy Lake Shore Drive. It will take us from North Avenue Beach to Lincoln Park Zoo. We'll visit farm animals from the U.S. Midwest, *arctic* animals from the far north, and some of my friends from Africa.

The zoo is free to visit. It opened in 1868. It is one of America's oldest zoos. I really feel at home here. There's a lion house, where the roars remind me of my homeland. African apes that I recognize swing from vine to vine. What are the chimpanzees doing? The chimps are eating from a termite mound, just like aardvarks do.

It might seem strange that lions and chimpanzees can live near skyscrapers. The zookeepers work hard to create comfortable homes for them. Workers at the zoo also study wildlife that lives in the city—bats, chipmunks, deer, and coyotes, to name a few.

Meet the president

The zoo is located in a huge park called Lincoln Park. Can you guess who it was named after? Abraham Lincoln, of course. He lived most of his life in Illinois, before becoming president of the United States in 1861. You can see a statue of him in the park.

Peggy Notebaert Nature Museum

I could spend all day in Lincoln Park. It gives my long, sensitive ears a break from the loud city noises—rumbling **L** trains and honking taxi horns. Let's stay in the park a while longer and visit the Peggy Notebaert Nature Museum. In the warm greenhouse, there are more than 1,000 butterflies. They fly around little pools, flowers, and tropical trees. One might land on your shoulder!

Ribbit! Hey, I hear the frogs in the marsh exhibit! Did you know this area used to be a **marsh** before the city was built? We can play with water displays at the museum, turning a river into a lake or building our own dam. We can even reverse the flow of a river, just as the city did with the Chicago River in 1900.

Up on the rooftop, we can look through binoculars at birds that live around North Pond. Then let's walk the nature trails outside to see if we can spot the birds up close.

Saving rare butterflies

Museum scientists help protect fragile, tiny *larvae*, or caterpillars, of rare butterflies during the winter. In spring, fully formed butterflies are released into the wild.

Sports town

Chicago is one of the world's great sports towns. Many of its professional teams have a long history, with several championships. But it is the loyalty of the fans that is most remarkable. Walk anywhere in Chicago, and you'll see someone proudly wearing a local team jersey or cap.

THE BEARS - FOOTBALL

Home field: Soldier Field
Game day traditions: Before the game, fans grill hot dogs and sausages and throw footballs around in the parking lot. It's called a tailgate party!

THE BULLS - BASKETBALL

Home court: United Center
Game day traditions: Before the game, the stadium goes dark. A loud theme song plays, and a light show flashes as the Bulls are introduced. The crowd goes wild.

THE BLACKHAWKS - HOCKEY

Home ice: United Center
Game day traditions: Before the puck is dropped, fans sing the national anthem at the top of their lungs. It's so loud you can't even hear the lead singer at the microphone.

Vamos! Chicago Fire

You might feel some of the excitement of Latin America at a Chicago Fire soccer game. Fans cheer on the team with songs and chants, sometimes in Spanish. *Vamos* means *let's go!* The Fire plays in the Chicago suburb of Bridgeview.

Baseball

Take me out to the ballgame! But wait. Which one? Chicago has two Major League Baseball teams. The rivalry, or competition, between them is strong! In Chicago, you're either a Cubs fan or a White Sox fan. It's the North Side of the city against the South Side! Let's start on the North Side.

The Chicago Cubs play in Wrigley Field, an old stadium with lots of traditions. The outfield wall is made of brick and covered in ivy. The huge outfield scoreboard is still changed by hand. When the Cubs win, the stadium flies a white flag with a blue *W* on it.

We can catch an **L** train outside Wrigley and take it to the South Side, to what locals call "Sox park." The Chicago White Sox play in a modern stadium with fun extras. Kids can swing away at balls in batting cages and run the bases after the game!

Wrigley Field

The hot dog is a treat we might enjoy at the ball park. If we go to the right vendor, we can get a hot dog Chicago style. It's got lots of toppings … and ketchup isn't one of them! The ingredients are:

1. A steamed, poppy seed bun
2. An all-beef hot dog
3. Mustard
4. Relish
5. Onions
6. Tomato wedges
7. Pickle
8. Spicy sport peppers
9. Celery salt

Blues

What's your favorite kind of music? Many **Chicagoans** love the blues. Blues is a kind of music started by African Americans. It has its roots in songs sung by people who were slaves and workers in farm fields. Blues songs are often about feeling *blue,* or sad.

In the 1900's, many African Americans from the American South moved north to Chicago. They were looking for jobs in the city's factories. Their musicians brought harmonicas, guitars, and the blues with them. They started using electric guitars, creating a style now known as

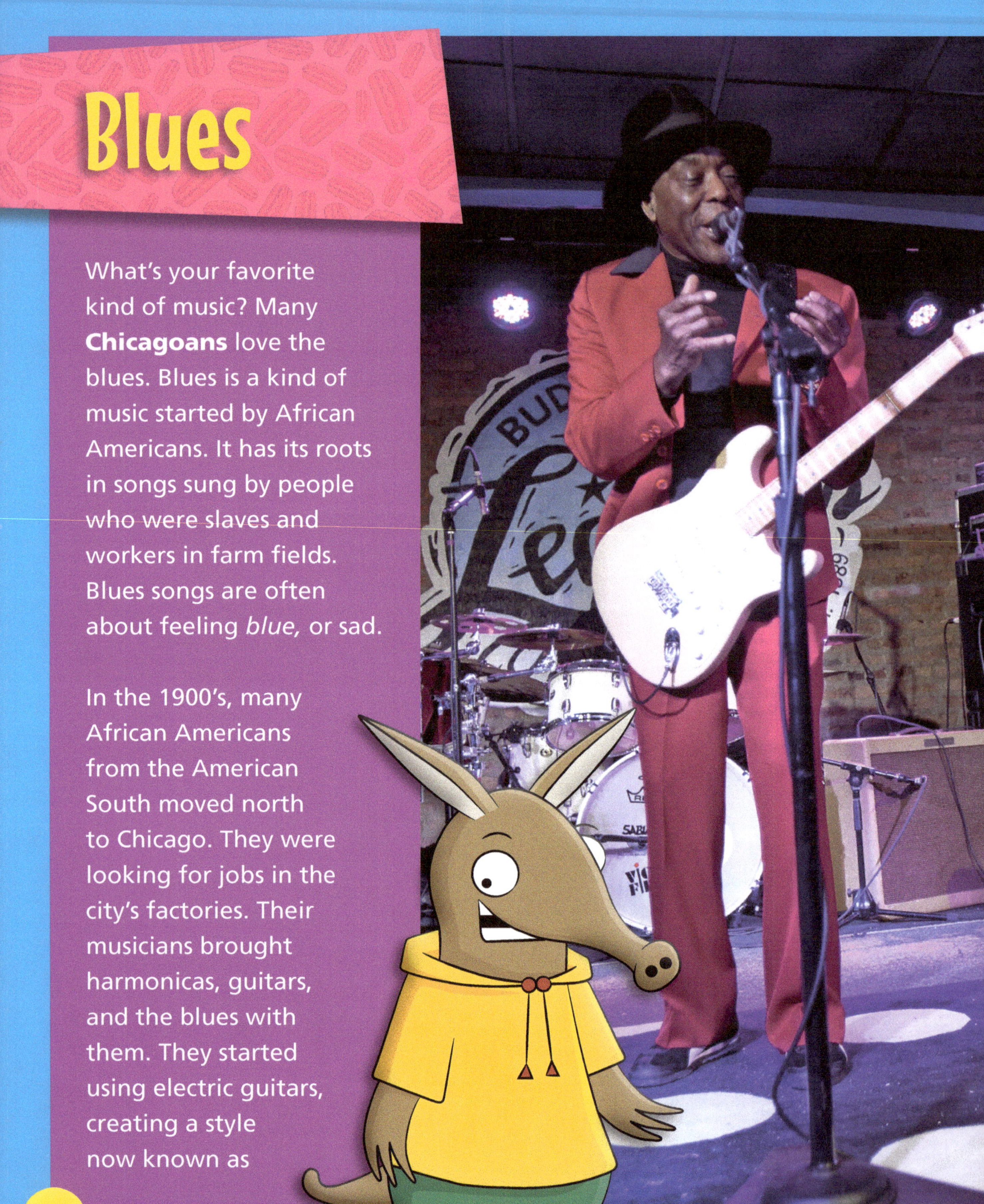

Chicago Blues. Since then, Chicago's South Side has been a popular place to hear some of the best blues musicians in the country.

Let's stop by Buddy Guy's Legends, a music club in the South Loop. Five days a week, kids like us are allowed in at lunchtime for the acoustic (pronounced, *uh KOO stihk*) show. That means the musicians play guitars that aren't electric. Look at all the different colored guitars on the wall! Each one belonged to a famous blues musician.

The Great Migration

From 1915 to 1970, more than 6 million African Americans moved from the rural South to such northern cities as New York City, Detroit, and Chicago.

Chicago eats

Are you hungry? Chicago has just about any kind of food. But some foods are unique to Chicago.

Perhaps the city's most famous food is its deep-dish pizza. Chicago-style pizza is probably thicker and cheesier than you're used to. It may measure 2 inches (5 centimeters) thick! The crust curves up the sides and holds heaps of toppings. The toppings are upside down compared with other pizzas. Chunky tomato sauce sits on the top, with cheese underneath. Wait a second— I don't see any tasty termites!

Are you a messy eater? You will be when you try an Italian beef sandwich. Extra meat will fall out onto the table. Delicious beef juice will drip onto your shirt! Even aardvarks need extra napkins. This sandwich was created in Chicago's Little Italy neighborhood, on the South Side, during the Great Depression (economic hard times in the 1930's). The people there sliced beef really thin and served it on thick slices of fresh bread.

Try it!

Deep-dish pizza was first made in Chicago in the early 1940's. Today many restaurants offer it, and Italian beef sandwiches, too.

Museum of Science and Industry

Let's catch a bus to Hyde Park, another South Side neighborhood. Here we can explore the Museum of Science and Industry. The museum has lots of interactive exhibits—things for us to do and try!

At the Science Storms exhibit, we can control a giant tornado spinning in the middle of the room. I feel like a wizard! Next, we can see a big fire burning inside a glass cube. Watch what happens when we add air or take it away. Imagine how the wind in Chicago could make a big fire even worse.

This grand building was built as part of the "White City," an attraction of the 1893 Columbian Exposition. The exposition was a huge celebration called a *world's fair.* It gave Chicago a chance to show off how well it had recovered from the Great Fire.

Want to go into a real *U-boat* (that's what Germans called a submarine)? The U-505 is from World War II, which was fought from 1939 to 1945. This *restored* (fixed-up) U-boat is on display in the museum's basement. We can find out how it was captured and take a peek inside.

Robie House

Let's take a walk through Hyde Park to see more **architecture.** This is the neighborhood of the world-famous University of Chicago. There are chapels and libraries in the fancy Gothic style. But there are also modern laboratories and arts centers.

There's one last thing we must see before our tour of Chicago ends: the Robie House. I hope you like long rectangles, because this home has thousands of them! Look for rectangles and other shapes in the bricks, the windows, the furniture, and the lamps.

Who came up with this unusual design? One of Chicago's most famous architects, Frank Lloyd Wright. He wanted to design a home that matched the wide plains found in this part of the country. He called the design "**prairie** style." See if you can spot all the long open rooms, the low roofs, and the natural colors. It looks like autumn in the Midwest. They were all part of Wright's plan for the house to blend into the landscape.

Where's the front door?

On Saturdays, kids lead some of the Robie House tours through the hidden front door and to secret places inside. If we head to the suburb of Oak Park, we can see more buildings Wright designed, including his own house.

Navy Pier
Lakefront Trail
Millennium Park
John G. Shedd Aquarium

Chicago River
Thanks for
exploring Chicago
with me. I hope to
see you soon!
Ayo

Glossary

architect, architecture *(AHR kuh tehkt, AHR kuh TEHK chur)* Architects are people who design buildings. Architecture is the art and science of designing buildings. It can also mean the style of buildings.

Chicagoan *(shih KAW goh uhn)* A person who lives in Chicago

L *(ehl)* Train lines that run on tracks built overhead, above street level. *L* is short for *elevated.*

engineer *(EHN juh NIHR)* A person who plans and builds engines, machines, roads, bridges, canals, forts, and similar things

Loop *(loop)* The heart of downtown Chicago. The city's elevated train tracks form a circuit, or loop, in the downtown area. The Loop is the neighborhood within and nearby this loop.

marsh *(mahrsh)* A kind of wetland

prairie *(PRAIR ee)* A region of flat or hilly land covered mostly by tall grasses

Acknowledgments

Cover © Sorbis/Shutterstock
Ayo artwork by Matthew Carrington

4-9   © Shutterstock
10-11   © Shutterstock; © Jiri Flogel, Shutterstock; Chicago Historical Society
12-13   Library of Congress; © Espiegle/iStockphoto; © Rudy Balasko, Shutterstock
14-19   © Shutterstock
20-21   © Tom Prout, iStockphoto; © Jason Patrick Ross, Shutterstock
22-23   © Steve Geer, iStockphoto
24-25   © Todd Bannor, Alamy Images; © Thomas Barrat, Shutterstock
26-27   © Felix Mizioznikov, Shutterstock
28-29   ©Shutterstock; © Songquan Deng, Shutterstock; © James Tung, iStockphoto
30-31   © Jason Lindsey, Alamy Images; © Joe Debiase, Dreamstime
32-33   © Jessica L Heiberger, Dreamstime
34-35   © Jerry Driendl, Getty Images; © Shutterstock
36-37   © Paul Natkin, WireImage/Getty Images; Public Domain
38-41   © Shutterstock
42-43   © Marek Lipka-Kadaj, Shutterstock; Library of Congress

Index

A

Adler Planetarium, 22-23
African Americans, 36-37
architecture, 9, 21, 42-43. *See also* skyscrapers
Art Institute of Chicago, 14-15

B

baseball, 34-35
basketball, 32
beaches, 26-27
Bean, The (sculpture), 16
blues, 36-37
breakwater barriers, 27
bridges, 9
Buckingham Fountain, 24, 25
Buddy Guy's Legends, 37
butterflies, 31

C

Chicago, 4-7
Chicago Bears, 33
Chicago Blackhawks, 32-33
Chicago Bulls, 33
Chicago Cubs, 34-35
Chicago Fire (team), 32
Chicago River, 8-9, 18, 25, 26, 45; flow of, 9, 30
Chicago White Sox, 34
Cloud Gate (sculpture), 16
Columbian Exposition, 19, 41
Crown Fountain, 16-17

E

875 North Michigan Avenue (building), 13
elevated trains, 14, 30, 34

F

Ferris, George W., 19
Ferris wheel, 18-19
Field Museum, 20, 21

food, 35, 38-39
football, 32
Fort Dearborn, 8

G

Grant Park, 17
Great Chicago Fire, 10-12, 41

H

hockey, 32-33
Home Insurance Building, 12
hot dogs, 35

J

Jenney, William Le Baron, 12
John G. Shedd Aquarium, 20-21, 44

L

L trains, 14, 30, 34
Lake Michigan, 9, 10; Lakefront Trail, 24-25, 44-45; shoreline, 17, 26-27
Lincoln, Abraham, 29
Lincoln Park, 29, 30
Lincoln Park Zoo, 28-29
Loop, The, 14
Lurie Garden, 16

M

Maggie Daley Park, 17
Magnificent Mile, 10
Michigan Avenue, 8, 10
Millennium Park, 16-17, 44
Museum Campus, 17, 20-24
Museum of Science and Industry, 40-41

N

Native Americans, 8
Navy Pier, 18-19, 24, 44
North Avenue Beach, 26-27
Northerly Island Park, 23

O

O'Leary, Mrs., 10

P

parks, 16-17
Peggy Notebaert Nature Museum, 30-31
pizza, 38-39
Potawatomi, 8
prairie style, 42

R

Riverwalk, 25
Robie House, 42-43

S

Seurat, Georges, 14
ships, 18-19, 27
Silver Spray (ship), 27
skyscrapers, 8, 12-13, 23
soccer, 32
sports, 32-35
Sue (dinosaur skeleton), 20
Sunday Afternoon on the Island of La Grande Jatte (painting), 14

U

U-boat display, 41
United Center, 32-33

W

Water Tower, 10-11
Willis Tower, 13
Windy City (name), 19
Wright, Frank Lloyd, 42-43
Wrigley Field, 34-35

For further reading

Books

Balliett, Blue. *The Wright 3.* New York: Scholastic Press, 2007.

Davis, Kathryn Gibbs. *Mr. Ferris and His Wheel.* Boston: HMH Books for Young Readers, 2014.

Hoberman, Mary Ann. *Mrs. O'Leary's Cow.* New York: Little, Brown and Company, 2007.

Layne, Deborah Dover. *W is for Windy City: A Chicago City Alphabet.* Ann Arbor, MI: Sleeping Bear Press, 2010.

Mullin, Michael. *Larry Gets Lost in Chicago.* Seattle: Little Bigfoot, 2010.

Websites

Architecture in Chicago
http://www.architecture.org/

Games and activities from the John G. Shedd Aquarium
http://www.sheddaquarium.org/Learning-Experiences/Fun-Games/

Guide to visiting Chicago
http://www.choosechicago.com